MINDFUL ENERGY

A Journey Of Transformation

By

SARAH HADLEY

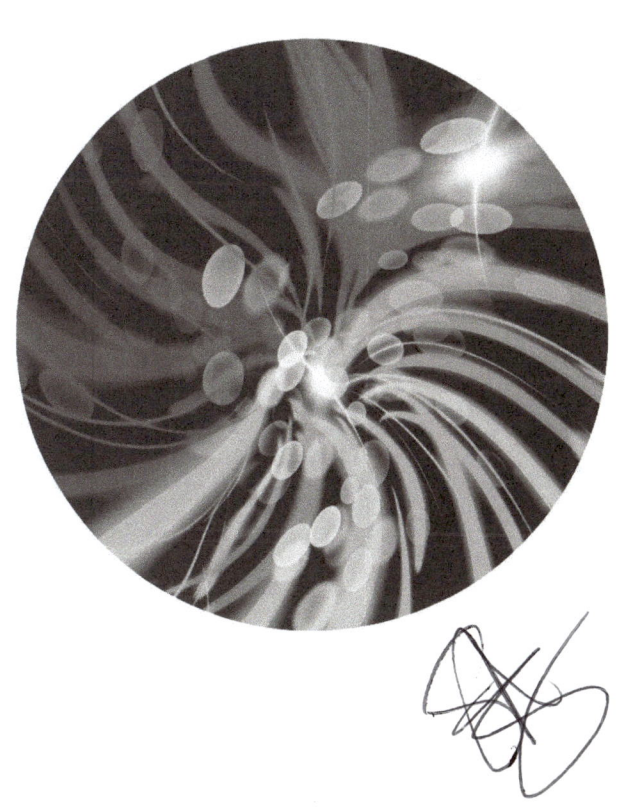

Copyright © 2016 by Sarah Hadley

All rights reserved. This book may not be reproduced in whole or in part, stored in a retrieval system, or transmitted in any form or by any means — electronic, mechanical, or other — without written permission from the publisher, except by a reviewer, who may quote brief passages in a review.

The material in this book is intended for educational purposes only. No expressed or implied guarantee of the effects of the use of the recommendations can be given or liability taken.

Cover design and interior illustrations by Sarah Gayle

First printing 2016

ISBN-13: 978-1537261355
ISBN-10: 1537261355

For bulk orders, requests, or to contact the author, visit www.mindfulenergybysarah.com

I am not what has happened to me. I am what I choose to become.

~ Carl Jung

What it Means to Live Though Mindful Energy

It is a method, a doing, a way of being. A merging of three parts: connection, presence, and energy — called to action by your intention and purpose. A practice that allows you to be clear about who you are, what you want, and how to get there. Mindful Energy is a simple, practical, and powerful method of attending to your thoughts, listening to your inner knowing, and being an active participant in the energy that influences all things. It is the act of neutralizing the power of destructive core beliefs, untangling yourself from the mess of expectations, and allowing you to show up for life, just as you are — with confidence and purpose.

By living through Mindful Energy you get to meet each experience as it comes, without attachment or expectation, allowing for space in which, acceptance, growth, and healing can happen. It is a moment by moment choice regarding how you build relationships with each and every aspect of your life. This book in your hand at this moment is not random. You were called to it because you are ready to live into your true purpose. Here is your invitation.

TABLE OF CONTENTS

Part One: To Be Present
Meeting the Moment - The Process of Observing Your Thoughts……………………7
Exercise: Observe Your Thoughts………….8
Exercise: Observe Your Surroundings…….11
Staying In Present Time……………………13
Exercise: Sitting With Discomfort………..18
Exercise: Let Go of the Need to Find Fault, Reason, and Familiarity……………….19

Part Two: Connection
Meet Clair, Your Guide to Intuition……….26
Exercise: Find Your Clair………………….30
Learning to Trust What You Know…………32
Exercise: Low Stakes Practice……………..35
Exercise: Higher Stakes Practice…………..37

Part Three: Energy
Energy Boundaries………………………….48
Exercise: Observe What's Going in and What's Going Out…………………………..51
Exercise: Anchor Yourself in the Present…53
Exercise: Claim Your Space……………….55
Energy Hygiene - How to Keep It Clean…57
Exercise: Choose A Cleansing Practice…..61

Pulling It All Together……………………..63
Mindful Energy Journal Section

To Be Present

Being present, or *mindful,* if you'd rather, is the simple act of meeting each experience as it comes. It's the process of observation. It's about being here and now, not rummaging around in the past, nor plotting and planning in the future. **It is *being*, without exacerbating nor minimizing what we are experiencing.**
Why is present time awareness important? Because no other time exists. All we ever have is right now.

Being present does not mean we have to sit in an arthritis-inducing position while in a cave in a faraway mountain. Being present means we meet each moment as it happens, whether we are working, sitting in traffic, playing sports, or shopping. In terms of mindfulness, it makes no difference *what* we are doing, we simply need to be fully aware and present *when* we are doing it.

When we engage in present time awareness and *observe* the experiences of life, we are able to disengage from dysfunctional attachments that have been created in the past and eliminate assumptions and anxieties about how the future will be.

Being present allows us to be fully open to all possibilities that exist in the universe. When we are not present — not mindful of what we are doing — we simply recreate what we *think* we know, keeping stuck patterns in place and missing out on what could be. When we are present, we always get to choose how we respond to any situation. We become in complete control of our experience. No longer will we be reactive and bounced around between emotions. When practicing present time awareness, you get to choose your experience.

When we are stuck in patterns, we end up floundering in life wondering why we keep experiencing the same disappointments in relationships, careers, and finances.

Being present, **meeting each experience as it comes**, automatically untangles us from expectations, attachments, and destructive beliefs. Don't misunderstand, it's not as if we can be present for a few minutes and unravel years worth of brain habits. Being present isn't a quick fix or a magic wand — it's a practice. It requires intention and action.

For thousands of years our brains have been trained to see all the negative and dangerous things. This made sense when we lived amongst lions, tigers, and poisonous plants. However, that wonderful evolutionary tool does not apply as much today. In fact, it often serves as a hindrance to connection and happiness. Observing and regulating our thought process allows us to go from seeing danger around every corner to seeing the possibility in all situations. Changing our neurology is possible, but it requires us to take action. We must show up for our thoughts and change the habit of anxiety-laden, negative thinking. **We must re-train the brain to consistently see the good.**

Good news! It gets easier. The more often we are present and choose one thought over another, the less challenging it becomes. It's a cycle.

Positive thoughts today increase the chance of positive thoughts tomorrow.

When we are present, we get to see how our thoughts stem from core beliefs and how observation — or awareness — changes the relationship with those destructive or inhibiting core beliefs. **Every** time you bring awareness to an experience you change the relationship with it, eliminating needless conflict, suffering, and stress. Every time you intentionally change your perspective from DANGER to possibility, you are actively working to evolve your thought process.

When we are not present, we experience our lives through the lens of past hurts and future anxieties, missing out on the vitality and possibly of what is ACTUALLY happening — we simply recycle old stuff by applying our past experiences to present time situations. Clinging to fixed (static) ideals keeps us from seeing possibility and opportunity. Because the possibility and opportunity will be obscured by fear and desire.

When we become present, we are able to engage in the current situation, free from expectations, destructive beliefs, fear, and anxiety, allowing ourselves to be open and receptive to the possibilities each moment brings. Through present time awareness, we get to finally see what is really happening, not just what we can identify with from the past. **In this space, this expanse of present time awareness, meaningful change happens.**

Being present allows for a more functional personal energy management and intuitive connection — as we will explore in later sections.

"Every fragment of self-talk is a little story in the head that goes around, and then you look at reality through the lens of the little story."   —Eckhart Tolle

Meeting the Moment : The Process of Observing Your Thoughts

Have you ever made the effort to observe your thoughts? It's a common scientific notion that we have somewhere around 60,000 thoughts during our waking hours. 60,000! That's a lot of thinking. Can you come up with even 50 of the thoughts you have had today? It's hard, isn't it? By observing your thoughts you begin the habit of meeting each moment as it comes, seeing it for what it is, not building attachments to it, and allowing any feeling to come and go as it needs. Our thoughts are powerful and create lasting changes within our brains and bodies. Leaving our thoughts unattended is like leaving a six-year old who has superpowers alone to manage the household — somewhat functional yet perfectly destructive.

When we don't like what's happening, we immediately try to change the circumstances. We do this by getting a new job, new hair, new relationship, or a new place to live. What we fail to understand is *we* are the common denominator in all of our experiences. Until we change who we *are*, at a fundamental, neurological, soul level, we will continue to *do* the same things — creating the same situations, over and over and over.

To make meaningful change we must change *ourselves* within the circumstance.

Exercise I Observe Your Thoughts

Similar to having a personal training coach who helps us achieve that next push-up or weight loss goal, it is helpful to put into place an external reinforcer that serves as our thought observation coach. This can be as simple as an alert on your phone. You can set a timer or calendar notification, or even download an app if you are using a smartphone. My favorite app is called 'Mindfulness Bell' from the Apple Store. Choose an alert that happens 4-6 times a day. Any more frequently and we begin to tune it out. If you are using a phone for the cuing, put this workbook down, grab your phone and set an alert or download an app. Each time the alert sounds, ask yourself, "Where am I?" then observe what you were thinking about. Do you have any emotions about what you were thinking about? Observe that. Once you have observed your thoughts and any subsequent emotions, take a deep breath and say, "Okay, here I am" bringing your attention back to present time. That's it. Do that over and over and over. Soon you will notice that an external cue is not as necessary and that you are spending more time in the present moment.

Example: My timed bell goes off, reminding me to be present. I ask, "Where am I?" and I find myself thinking about an argument I had with a friend earlier in the week. I observe that I have really been rehashing what she said and how she said it and what I should have said. I observe that I feel angry, anxious, and a bit indignant about this argument. I take a deep breath (or two or three) and say, "Here I am," bringing my attention back to present time. Notice that I do not attempt to change what I am feeling in this example. I don't notice that I am feeling angry and anxious only to try and change it, or resist it in some way. I simply see it for what it is. **This process validates the feeling, without assigning meaning and then allows it to move along when it is finished being experienced.** We do not find meaning through our experiences — or what we *do*, we find meaning through who we *are*.

Exercise I Observe Your Surroundings

I am part of my surroundings. Remember the example I gave with observing thoughts, in which I was rehashing an argument I'd had with a friend? After observing my thoughts I began to observe my physical self, I noticed that I was tense and, until I took a few deep breaths, my breathing pattern was very shallow and somewhat fast. My brow was furrowed and I was feeling a bit grouchy. I was feeling all of this while sitting on my porch — a place I usually feel happy and relaxed — doing nothing but flipping through a magazine. My present time circumstance did nothing to warrant my physical experience of tension and anger. My present time circumstance was actually quite peaceful. All of my physical distress was in response to my *thoughts* about something that wasn't even happening. See how that works?

The first place to observe your surroundings is within yourself — in your physical body. Start with the crown of your head and move downward, mentally scanning in all directions, making note of any tightness, tingling, warmth, cold, pain, or fatigue.

Then move outward observing the physical space around you. Spend at least five minutes observing in detail the space you are currently in. Notice textures, colors, contrasts, objects big and small. Then observe how your body feels within this space. Is the space you are in creating comfort? Is it creating distress or distraction? Does it *feel* like a pleasant place to be? Using the same process of observing your thoughts, simply notice what is happening without trying to figure out where it came from, what it means, or what to do with it. (I will address that compulsion later)

Staying in Present Time

Okay. Okay. You get it. Observe your thoughts. Great. Observed. *Now what?* You see them; now what do you *do* with them?! Be wary of falling into this trap.

We want to immediately go from observing our thoughts — present time — to finding the origin of any distressing thought (past) and wanting to know what to do with it (future).

See what happened there? We observed our thoughts, found distress, and instead of staying present with it, we jump right back OUT of present time rummaging around in the past to find its origin and then leaping over the present time — oh so nimble, oh so quick — right into the future to find a fix. We do this with positive thoughts as well, it just unfolds in a slightly different way. When we observe our thoughts and find something pleasant, we have a tendency to leap out of the present time, not necessarily to find a fix as with the negative thoughts, but in attempt to grasp onto *all the happy things*, so they **never** go away. If you remember from the previous section, our brains are wired to seek pleasure and avoid pain. This desire to grasp, to attempt make static that which *will* change, creates a dysfunctional attachment certain to cause pain — because nothing is static. Everything will change. **In effect, we trade short moments of pleasure for extended periods of pain, all the while missing out on being present with what *is*.** When we are not present, we are not truly engaging with and appreciating the things that bring us joy. We miss out because we are attempting to keep *all the happy things* with us. All the time. Can you see the problem here?

The compulsion to fix or to make static is the antithesis of actually experiencing something. Contrary to our pop culture beliefs, sitting in present time with something *is* the fix. It *is* the way to keep *all the happy things* with us for as long as they exist and allow us to be available for *all the new happy things* when they arrive.

Seeing things for what they are, as they are, diminishes the negative impact individual events have in your life, allowing you to experience more happiness and less stress.

Why is a past event still around and effecting you? Because you didn't fully experience it and let it go the first time. You denied it or made it into some sort of fuel source or protective mechanism and stuck it away on a nice and tidy shelf inside of yourself to access whenever you desire justification, motivation, or protection.

We are in the habit of reacting to an occurrence rather than experiencing it for what it is, just as it is. When we are in a reactionary space we spend a tremendous amount of energy checking our mental catalog of life experiences, looking for similar hurts or reaffirming belief patterns, and then jump right over present time — where life is actually happening — looking towards the future, devising multiple (and usually complex) scenarios on how we are going to avoid pain or protect our precious self-image. Spending time and energy in the mental catalog of *all the awful things* is depressing. Conversely, spending time and energy conjuring up complex scenarios that rarely ever come to be, creates unnecessary anxiety. For example: I am heading out the door to go to work and I get a text from my boss asking me to meet him in his office when I get there. This is all that has actually happened so far. I get a text from my boss. And then my brain kicks into high gear. I begin to mentally review my previous week's work performance and anticipating any and all possible outcomes. Did I get all my paperwork in on time? I wonder if *that* client complained, she complains about everything. She's such a grouchy hag. What is her deal anyway? Did I put in the order for supplies like I was supposed to on Friday? God, I hope this isn't about budget cuts. They let Suzy and Mark go from the other department just last week. What if I get laid off? What would I do? How would I make it? Who else would hire me? How could I tell my husband something like that? How do you break the ice there? "Hey, babe. How was your day? Did you enjoy eating lunch at the restaurant? Because you will have to stop doing that because I lost my job. Because of me, you can't enjoy nice lunches."

Maybe Marcie is gossiping about me again, she has *no* sense of humor at the office. Is she like that at home, too? I can't imagine coming home to that every day.

On and on my brain goes until I reach the office. I'm sweaty, a little panicked, and glaring at Marcie. I arrive at the boss's door, he looks up from his desk and says, "I'm going on vacation for two weeks, can you keep this orchid in your office?" Pointing to the plant on his shelf. "Orchids are kind of finicky and I think it will do best in there while I'm gone."

Exercise | Sitting With Discomfort

If you find discomfort while observing your thoughts, resist the urge to flee from present time. Intentionally stay present. Breathe and breathe again (this helps calm the nervous system that is sending false fight/flight signals) and observe any thoughts, feelings, or emotions related to this discomfort. When you have the urge to leap to the future to fix it (because, for the love of god, just make it go away!), breathe and stay present. Or, when you want to rummage in the past to find out WHO DID THIS TO ME, breathe and intentionally stay present. Observe the urges to avoid being present. Sit. Breathe. And when the feeling begins to dissipate, let it go. Thank it if you must, that can be helpful. Even when dysfunctional, we keep things around for a reason — so thank it, and **let it go**.

Exercise I Let Go of the Need to Find Reason, Fault, and Familiarity

What was once a protective mechanism, protecting us from mortal danger, the habit of constantly scanning our environment and situations for danger and similar pain, has now become a barrier to our happiness. We are in the habit of rummaging in the past for two main reasons: to find familiar situations in order to identify and understand what we are currently facing or to avoid a similar pain. We do this in particular when trying to make decisions and our time, money, heart, or reputation is dependent on the outcome. If we are not intentionally present, we habitually scan the past for similar situations or hurts — so that we can figure out what we are doing and how to not get hurt doing it.

When trying to problem solve and rationalize our way through the decision making process, we scan for familiarity. If we can't find a similar situation that is logged in our mental catalog of *all the things*, we end up saying, "I can't possibly see how this would work," and not moving forward. Or, we rummage around, find a similar hurt, take that out of the past, and apply it to the current situation — *even if it doesn't apply to what is actually happening in present time.*

What to do about this? Validate what has happened and be open for things to be different. Observe, without judgement, what has occurred — no matter how great or nasty. But don't bring that experience into the present time and apply it to what is currently happening. Let the present time unfold without applying old hurts. Hurt and pain is what we will primarily look for — that's the protective mechanism. We constantly try to mitigate damage. Asking ourselves, *how can this hurt me? What is this going to cost me?*

To get out of this dreary loop, move into the world of **and**. That happened *and* I'm open to things being different. I recognize *that*, **and** I'm open to the unlimited possibilities that are available. I am open to what can be. I am willing to show up when it comes. **I meet each experience as it comes, see it for what it is, release the need to rummage in the past to find past hurts or jump into the future to conjure all outcomes. I sit in the present meeting each thing as it comes, remaining open to all the possibilities of the universe,** *and* **I will show up when it happens.**

Connection

Everything that we interact with, seen or unseen, has a message attached. Some are simple, others are complex, but they all carry a message.

Can you hear it? Are you listening?

Our intuition is fed and fostered by connecting to the vast amount of information that flows all around us. *Intuition is connection.* Intuition provides valuable information that, if used, allows for clarity, ease, and possibility in your life. When we connect, listen, trust, and act, we are able to see the bigger picture, a picture that holds possibilities that we cannot fathom through reason alone. Intuition takes us beyond what we can comprehend through our traditional five senses and what we can scan for in our catalog of *all the things*. Intuition is simply reading the energy that is present. When we are present, connected, and listening, we are able to hear the knowing of the energy that is all around us.

Connect — Good news! Everyone has access. We are hardwired to receive the subtle energy messages of intuition. This information rides on the waves of subtle energy currents that our bodies are wired to receive. We already have everything we need. There is no special thing that needs to be done in order to access or activate — no encrypted wifi password, no secret handshake, no special tools.

You already are and always have been connected.

Everyone is naturally intuitive. Granted, some have stronger abilities than others, but we all have it. All of us are receivers, but not all of us listen.

Listen — So, I'll start by answering the question almost everyone asks: How do I know what I am hearing is my intuition and not just my thoughts — or something else? When you tune in, intentionally connecting to the subtle energy, listening to your intuition — you will *feel* it. It won't be a thought that remains in your head; it will be a *knowing*, connected with a feeling that

23

permeates all of your body. Intuition is subtle, calm and solid. You feel an assurance with intuition.
Why listen? Why not?? Why would we leave all of this valuable information on the table? Who reads only every third page of instructions while trying to figure something out? That would be absurd. So is not listening to our intuition.
When we ignore our intuition, we are leaving valuable information on the table.

Trust — Here's the deal, you already know that you know what you know. The real problem is trust. We don't trust what we *know* is true. We doubt the intuition that comes in, second guessing ourselves. Saying, "that can't be what that was; I can't know that," especially if the information is somehow contrary to what appears logical or reasonable to our brains. All too often we have had our intuition — our inner knowing — denied by others. Our culture has become uncomfortable with *knowing*, instead seeking shallow comfort and satisfaction in events that are rational, logical, and concrete.

Learning to trust what you *know* is often the biggest hurdle.

Act — Act upon the information you get. Be reasonable; it would make no sense to ignore our other equally important senses like hearing and sight. If I were to be standing at the street corner preparing to cross, my best use of sense would be my ears and eyes — just like they teach us in primary school — stop, look, and listen. I wouldn't close my eyes and attempt to intuit a safe time to cross. However, if I looked and listened and determined by using those senses that it was safe to cross and I stepped off the curb only to have a clear intuitive message of "WATCH OUT!," I would step back on the curb and look around, maybe even waiting a minute before attempting to cross again. I'm saying trust your intuition, not throw out your other useful senses.

Meet Clair, Your Guide to Intuition

We are all wired to receive intuitive information and we receive that information through different channels. In this section I will introduce the four main channels, the 'Clairs' — Clairvoyant, Clairsentient, Claircognizant, and Clairaudient. Clair means clear, therefore the words literally translate to clear seeing, clear feeling, clear knowing, and clear hearing. There are more ways to receive intuition than those mentioned here, but these four are by far the most common. You can have more than one and you can certainly develop more than one way, but you will have a natural/strongest type. Start with that one to find your easiest Clair connection.

Clairvoyant means clear seeing. Clairvoyants actually see the information they are getting intuitively, which involves receiving information through pictures or images. These pictures or images may be symbolic or literal. For example, if I ask a clairvoyant what color the next car through the traffic light will be, and they intuit "red", they will *see* a red car, the color red, or maybe even the word red. Or, if I were to ask, "where did I leave my wedding ring?" and they intuit "at the kitchen sink", they may *see* a picture of dishes — rather than the literal space of the kitchen sink. Each group of Clair's tend to share common characteristics, some of those specific to clairvoyants are: being easily distracted, creative and artistic, clearly remembering a place they've only been once, sees the big picture, but can miss small details, and can easily construct items from seemingly complicated instructions. During conversation, they will be likely to say, "I see what you are saying."

Clairsentient means clear feeling, and alternately referred to as an empath. They largely experience intuitive knowing through feeling. They *feel* what is going on around them. They feel the emotions, feelings, and weight of other people, places, and things. Clairsentients can physically feel the pain, distress, anxiety, depression, and fear of others around them. They generally pair their incoming information with another Clair, finding accuracy in the answer that *feels* right. For example, a clairsentient will intuit that a red car will be the next through the light by seeing, knowing, or hearing the answer — they know it's accurate by the way it *feels*. Common characteristics of clairsentients include, feeling overwhelmed in crowds, having frequent intense displays of emotion, finding themselves in healing/caregiving roles, having a difficult time watching sad, scary, or violent movies, being excellent listeners and storytellers, as well as good cooks. During conversation, clairsentients will be likely to say, "I feel you."

Claircognizant means clear knowing. These folks just *know* what they know. When asked a question, they simply know the answer. Information seems to just pop into their heads. Theirs is a complete knowing that happens quickly, allowing them to think fast on their feet and tend to be great problem solvers and decision makers. Claircognizants also have the ability to learn new things quickly — often without instruction, as well as find themselves drawn to intellectual and analytical stimulation. During conversation, claircognizants will be likely to say, "I know what you are saying."

Clairaudient means clear hearing. Their answers and information come in the form of sound. Using the above example of the car, clairaudients would *hear* the word "red". They often find answers among songs or music, and have the ability to hear between the lines — hearing what is left unsaid or unwritten, or hearing what has been said outside of the range of what their ears can pick up. Clairaudients are good conversationalists, storytellers, and quickly know when a lie is being told. You will often find them talking to themselves and require quiet solitude fairly frequently. During conversations, clairaudients will be likely to say, "I hear you."

Exercise | Find Your Clair

Begin to pay attention to how you are bringing in information by using an intuition journal. Simply make note of how you came to know what you know. Did you picture it? Hear it? Know it? Feel it? Remember, you are likely to have episodes of all four Clairs, but you are looking for the most frequent and most clear for now.

Clairvoyant (clear seeing)

Clairsentient (clear feeling)

Claircognizant (clear knowing)

Clairaudient (clear hearing)

Learning to Trust What You Know

All of this information will do you no good if you don't trust it, because if you don't trust it, you won't use it. The most common question that I am asked as soon as I say this is, "How do I know what's my intuition and what is my thought? How do I know I'm not imagining things?"

For the sake of ease and simplicity, I will lump things into two categories: **intuition** and **everything else**. Put ego, thoughts, reason, and imagination into the everything else category. There's no real need to separate them out for this because they are all NOT intuition. That's all you really need to know.

So, then what *is* intuition?
Intuitive messages are energy messages that have become conscious — providing information in regards to where we are and where we need to go, telling us where we are in relationship to others (connection), and how to get to our next destination. **It is the simple act of paying attention to and understanding the messages**

held in the energy around us. I like to think of intuition as cosmic Googling. I get to ask questions that provide me with information and I also get "suggestions" that pop up as I am doing other things. Much like Google, what I ask and how I ask matter in terms of what I will find. And, much like "suggestions" that pop up, what we ask for, what we listen to, and what we "click" on intuitively, shapes what we are exposed to.

As I said before, we *all* have intuitive ability. But, if we haven't been attending to it, intentionally cultivating and using it, we need to start with the basics in order to foster its power, accuracy, and most importantly our trust in it.

First, you need to distinguish the difference between intuition and 'everything else.'

The voice of intuition is subtle and solid. There is no fear or desire attached to this voice. **It just is.** In contrast, the voice of everything else will be loud, pushy, and will provoke a thought/feeling of fear or desire.

When asking for something, **intuition will always be your first answer.** The second answer — which will be close on the heels of the first — will be the voice of 'everything else'. The voice that challenges the *knowing* you've had. The voice of 'everything else' will demand proof, or go into a dialogue of rationalization or justification. The voice of intuition does not do that.

The voice of intuition says, "This is what is." The voice of 'everything else' says, "Well, but..."

The voice of intuition feels calm, solid, and clean in your body, whereas the voice of 'everything else' feels tight, anxious, and dense.

Doubt is the voice of 'everything else.' Certainty is the voice of intuition. **The voice of doubt, reason, and logic has its place. Its place is not in place of our intuition.**

Exercise I Low Stakes Practice

It's time to use your intuition in your daily life. Ask questions, and pay attention to the FIRST answer you get.

No matter how silly or improbable it may seem, redirect the urge to examine the answer under the microscope of 'everything else.' Simply listen to and record your answer. As you're doing this, *feel* the difference between the first answer (intuition) and the second answer (everything else). When you take the time to really pay attention to the differences in these two voices, not only to how they sound but also how they *feel*, you will be able to distinguish them from one another with ease.

Put objects into a lunch sized paper bag that are the same size, but have a different color or symbol on them. For example, you can use marbles, domino's, paper clips (colored ones), Legos or runes. Reach into the bag, grab ahold of one of the objects and use your intuition to determine the color or symbol. Before pulling it out, ask "what color is this?" or "what symbol is this?" Pay attention to the *first* answer. You can apply this same concept in a number of ways — grab a handful of coins, intuit how many there are, how many of each coin, and/or the total value of the coins. Watch passing cars, intuit the color of the next car through the traffic light or to turn the corner. You get the idea.

Exercise | Higher Stakes Practice

It's time to intuit things that will cost you something, such as time, money, or credibility. Using the same process as you did with the marbles and coins, begin to intuit the best route to drive to work, home, or during errands. Ask which road will have less traffic. And then try it out.

If you are looking to make a purchase, outside of the typical grocery and household items, say, for example you need a new dishwasher, intuit which store will have exactly the type you want and for the best price — for you. **Being specific matters** when asking for intuitive answers. If you were to just ask for the best price, it could be the best price for the store, which could mean a greater expense for you.

Here's a great example of the benefit of being specific that happened while I was writing this book. I was teaching one of my students how to practice using her intuition, using exercises similar to the ones in this section. She came up with the idea to intuit how many hangers she would need to hang up all the shirts that were in the pile of laundry heaped on her bed. As she was telling me this during one of our sessions, she started out by saying, "I don't think I'm doing this right." I asked why she didn't think so and she proceeded to tell me this: she asked for how many hangers she would need to hang up all her shirts and pulled out six hangers. She then began to sort the laundry. This is when she tells me, "I hung up all my shirts, but had two sweaters and a dress left. I'm off somehow." I began to laugh. I said, "So, you had six hangers for six shirts?" At this point it began to dawn on her, she didn't ask for the amount of hangers needed to hang up *everything*, she asked for the amount of hangers she would need to hang up her *shirts*. She was 100% accurate in what she asked.

I can't emphasize this enough — **be as specific as possible when asking for intuitive information.**

Also, pay attention to nudges that take you in unexpected directions. You never know what's around the corner until you venture to look.
Ask clarifying questions, of your intuition and of those around you. Make sure you are being as specific as possible.
Still not finding what you are looking for? I guarantee it's not because your intuition is broken or not good enough. Sometimes we are not to know certain things for reasons that fall in line with our soul purpose and divine plan. Other times, we simply aren't asking the right questions. **Don't give up, be persistent. Keep practicing.**

Here's an example that happened to me. I was helping a friend find a watch for his wife. He had an idea in mind and I had a place in mind (my intuition told me where to go). We got there and looked at what they had in the case, but nothing fit what he was looking for. So, I asked my intuition again, "Is this watch here?" And I got a YES!

At this point it would have been really easy to allow my 'everything else' voice to pipe up demanding to know just *where* this watch is, if it's not in the case, and terminate our mission. Luckily, I've been at this for a while. *Knowing* that the watch was there, despite what we could see, I asked the jeweler if they had anything in the back that fit our description. His face brightened and said, "Wait a minute!" as he opened a locked cupboard. Pulling out a watch box the jeweler said, "I had forgotten about this; it was a special order that has been sitting here for months because it was never picked up." He opened the box and it was the exact watch my friend was looking for.

No matter how silly or improbable it may seem, redirect the urge to examine your intuition under the microscope of 'everything else.' Simply listen to and record what comes in. As you're doing this, *feel* the difference between the first answer (intuition) and the second answer (everything else). When you take the time to really pay attention to the differences in these two voices, not only to how they sound but also how they feel, you will be able to distinguish them from one another with ease.

Use your intuition, it works. **Practice** it, it's like a muscle that needs regular exercise. **Have fun** with it — because it's super fun. **Trust** it.
You know what you know.

Energy

There is an undeniable life force that flows through us, connecting us to not only the universe around us but, more importantly, to each other. This life force has been called many things over time: prana, chi, spirit, river of life — whatever name resonates with you, call it that. And know that you have influence over your own life force: you can direct it, protect it, and enhance it.

Not caring for, or not knowing how to care for our energy body leaves us vulnerable to physical, emotional, mental, and spiritual dysfunction.

Any falsehood we think or speak creates resistance in our energy body, or as I like to call it, 'the rub'. Much like the blood in our circulatory system, energy needs to flow uninhibited in order to do its job. 'The rub' prevents that from happening and creates energy blockages — trapping too much energy in one area, leaving a deficit in another. All of which can lead to physical ailments (especially illnesses related to inflammation or degeneration), difficulty regulating emotions, lack of mental acuity (brain fog), and spiritual disconnection. Every time we think or say something that is not true *to us*, we create a rub. It is important for good energy health to create the habit of speaking and thinking your truth, even when it is uncomfortable, even if it's only to yourself.

> "You are responsible for the energy you bring into this space."
> Dr. Jill Bolte Taylor

When you attend to your energy body, you open yourself for clearer, more direct intuition, leaving you with a calm, directed force in which to apply to all areas of your life. Calm directed energy provides the foundation for increased focus, motivation, and overall well-being.
Like the other methods in this workbook, there are no special tools needed. You have everything you need already, right here. Managing energy is a natural process; we are designed to do it.

There is a *ton* of reading material out there on the energy body. So, rather than go into depth here about what it *is*, I want to spend this time and space talking about what it *does* and how it *feels*. If you want to study more about the energy body, I highly recommend the work of Cyndi Dale, Donna Eden, Anodea Judith, and Caroline Myss.

So, on to how it feels. It is our energy body that emits and receives subtle energy signals, signals that carry important information — signals that will be muffled by the rub. It is our energy body talking when we walk into a room and immediately feel a weight, leaving us wondering, "What happened here?!" It is the same with the immediate reactions we have meeting someone, when we are drawn close or repelled away, outside of any rationalization our brain can come up with — and *will* try; remember the 'everything else' from the last chapter? We have this immediate feeling, this immediate *knowing* — that is our energy body giving us messages. Sound familiar? Intuition is the ability to clearly read the energy around us.

Where is it and what does it look like?

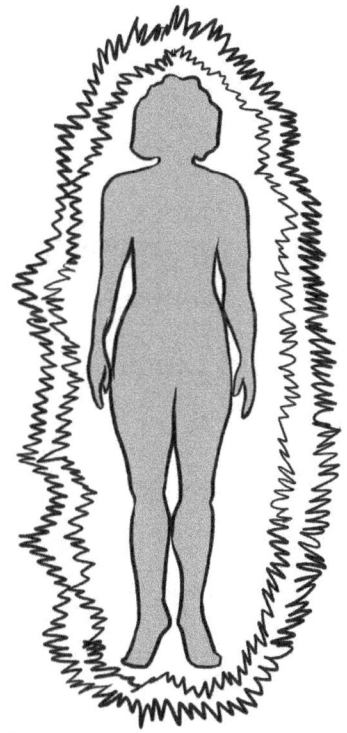

Again, for the sake of keeping this book simple and direct, I will give you a basic visual.
This subtle energy flows through every cell in our body and extends out approximately two to three feet from our skin, in every direction.
Much like our skin, the energy body is exposed to the elements. In this case it's not only the elements of weather, but also the elements of our surroundings. Our energy body is exposed to the energy of all other things — most importantly for

this subject, the energy of emotions, feelings, thoughts, beliefs and expectations. It is our energy body that interacts with the cloud of frustration coming off of our co-worker or the weight of expectation that is leaning on us from a loved one.

Because our energy body is exposed to the elements, it can get dirty with what I call energetic debris. Bits and pieces of this debris can get stuck to us. This isn't a big deal, just stuff that needs to be cleaned off — kind of like a grimy, bug laden windshield. The grime and bugs aren't out to get you; they are simply a consequence of driving through the environment, but they *will* still obstruct your vision. Just wash it off. Squirt squirt, wipe wipe: simple.

Our energy body can become disconnected. At times, we become disconnected from our source of nourishment which is the natural world and the spiritual world. When disconnected, our energy bodies become malnourished and, much like our physical bodies, when that happens we can experience the following — apathy, hopelessness, mood swings, sadness, restless or excessive sleep, chronic fatigue, disordered eating, agitation, and poor concentration.

Our energy body can be plugged into the wrong things — wrong meaning things that do not serve *our* soul purpose — which can result in confusion, lack of direction, feeling stuck, unable to move forward with a job or marriage, and shame. Or, our energy body can have someone else plugged into it, which can create internal conflict, a feeling of living off-purpose, chronic fatigue, chronic pain, and disorganized thoughts.

It can also be overcharged. This happens when we are taking in too much. Too much work, too much expectation, too many feelings and emotions from other people, which produces anxiety, fatigue, restlessness, irritability, compulsive thoughts, excessive worry, insomnia, nausea, and poor concentration.

Be energetically receptive for change by consciously choosing what you plug into.

Energy Boundaries

Okay, so we have this energy body that interacts with everything around us, sends messages, and can plug into other things. How do we maintain good energy boundaries? How do we keep our energetic hands to ourselves?? And, how do we keep others' energetic debris off of us?

First, and maybe foremost, is awareness. The simple act of knowing we have an energy body and the subsequent intention to keep it to ourselves, has a beneficial effect. **Attention and intention matters.** Setting an intention is a focused commitment. Pay attention. Using the techniques learned in the chapter on present time awareness, observe what infringes on your energy boundaries and where you infringe on others. What does this look like? It could be carrying home stress and anxiety from the office, meeting with a person and leaving that meeting feeling *their* feelings, getting sick in the same way of those around you, seeking out certain people or situations in order to change how you feel, or feeling drawn to anxiety and drama. When we find ourselves at the constant hub of stress, anxiety, drama, and illness, we must ask ourselves what we are doing to attract ourselves to those situations. **In all of your life circumstances, *you* are the common denominator.**

Destructive core beliefs and negative thought habits can erode our energy boundaries. If my thought habit says, "I will never find love," or "People like me don't deserve good things," those thought habits will poke holes in our boundaries, much like a moth eating fabric. When

these holes are present, intrusive energy from others is allowed to creep in. Like finds like, so the intrusive energy will act to reinforce your self-defeating thought habits. We end up making all of our life decisions based on these destructive thought habits and intrusive energy.
Yuck, right? I know.

The good news is, we are in complete control of our energy boundaries. We don't have to let anything in that we don't want to.

Exercise I Observe What's Coming in and What's Going Out.

Our energy follows our thoughts. If I am rehashing and rehearsing an incident at work, my energy will join in on the action. Remember the past/present exercise in the previous chapter? It's like that. Our energy leaves present time and goes to a land of make believe — a land filled with fret and worry. This weakens our energy boundaries and leaves us exhausted.

Pick three common life areas, such as the workplace, significant other, finances, parenting, school, friend groups or religious/spiritual group, and observe thoughts, feelings, and reactions you have when interacting with any of the three you've chosen. Pay attention to thought habits by asking "What am I thinking?" Take note of physical feelings like an upset stomach, headache, tightness, or fatigue, and intuitive or 'gut' feelings — or does your selected life area leave you feeling light, expansive, and relaxed? What message is the energy surrounding the chosen people and/or circumstances trying to convey? Keep a record here, in a journal, or on a digital device — it doesn't matter. Choose a method that fits for you and one that you will be most likely to follow through with. Record the messages you are getting around these experiences, and remember to *trust* what you know, go with the first answer, and ignore the 'everything else.'

Exercise I Anchor Yourself in the Present.

Present time is where our energy thrives, allowing it to nourish, recharge, and cleanse our whole self. Our energy body knows what to do, just like our circulatory system knows the exact way to deliver the vital building blocks for our physical health. What we have to do is, keep the system clean from debris, free from excessive 'rubs', and stay aligned with our soul purpose.

Take four or five deep breaths. In through the nose, blowing out through the mouth — this calms our nervous system. Say, "Okay, here I am," bringing all parts of yourself to the present. Take four to five more breaths, while staying present. Notice the feeling you have in this space.

Is it calm, focused, and powerful? If not, take a few more breaths and repeat, "Okay, here I am." Made it there? Great. In this space choose an anchor word. Choose a word that will bring you back to this space with nothing more than intention and a deep breath or two. Visualize what that word looks like in your space. People have chosen tree, rooted, grounded, solid — you can even use anchor. Practice this once or twice a day so that your thought habits become aligned with the internal and external circumstances.

To review: breathe, say, "Okay, here I am," while setting the intention to bring all your energy back to you. Notice the calm, focused power in and around you. Say your anchor word. Visualize that word merging into your space of present time awareness, a space where all your energy is present and accounted for.

This word will serve you well when you begin to feel unhinged, ungrounded, and intruded upon. Take a deep breath, say or think your word, and it will bring you back to this space.

Exercise | Claim Your Space

Much like creating physical boundaries with fences and cubicles, we can create energetic boundaries that will discourage people from coming into our space. This comes in the form of a simple visualization. When you walk into a room visualize you are a King or Queen with ornate and expensive flowing robes and gowns. Gowns and robes that no one would dare touch or step on because that would be disgraceful and rude. When a King or Queen enter a room, everyone else moves aside, creating space in which to pass. It is not an aggressive measure, nor an entitled one, it is simply an act of respect for royal boundaries.

Visualize yourself in these robes. Doing so enforces the attention and intention of maintaining energetic boundaries without infringing on or being abrasive to anyone else.

Energy Hygiene — How to Keep It Clean

We talked briefly in the opening section about energetic debris. These are bits and pieces of mismanaged energy that belong to other people, places, things, and circumstances. It is similar to pollen or dust floating around, and you walk through it collecting it on your energy body. In and of itself, it's mostly inert. However, without regular cleansing it can cause problems. **When our energy field is clouded with debris, it makes it difficult to *see* and interpret the energetic world around us.** And when we do see it, it will be through the lens of the debris we have collected. We begin to make decisions out of character, feel emotions that are not ours, take on illnesses that did not originate from a bacterial or viral intrusion. When we walk around with a dirty energy body we stop living our purpose and simply react to the energy that is stuck to us. We are responsible for the energy we bring into a space. It is our responsibility to bring a clean, vibrant energy — not a dark, sludgy, disease-laden energy.

Would you tromp through a neighbor's house with muddy boots? Or visit a sick relative in the hospital knowing you had whooping cough? Probably not. Take care of your energy the same way you take care of physical and spatial hygiene. We wash our hands and wear gloves when handling body fluids, sweep and mop our floors, launder our clothes, and wipe down the shopping cart handle at the grocery store. Yet, because you've been largely unaware of the workings of the energy body, you essentially tromp through the house with muddy boots, ingest all the debris in the environment, absorb everyone's feelings and problems, and are left to wonder why you aren't feeling vibrant and at ease — which is an incredibly frustrating and defeating place to be for those who have been earnestly working towards positive growth.

Ways to clean your energy:
Smudging: Use your intuition to find a good smudge for you (because I know you've been practicing and are an expert intuitive by now).

Sage is a common one and really effective. I prefer a sweetgrass and cedar mix. Smudge around your physical body, including the bottoms of your feet. It may be helpful to have someone help thoroughly get your back. You can smudge your space too. Regular smudging of your office, bedroom, car etc. is helpful in keeping the energy fresh and clean of stagnant energy. Smudging sprays are also available for those who cannot or choose not to burn something.

Baths/showers: I love love love hot showers. So, I use this time (for me, once a day) to clean all the energetic debris off of me. All I have to do while washing with soap is to set the intention that all energetic debris will wash away too. Salt baths are *amazing* and cleansing. I would recommend taking a salt bath at least once a week, using Epsom Salts — you can find them at most stores.

Brush it off: I can't help but to queue up Taylor Swift's song 'Shake it off' in my head while writing this. Physically brush off energy. Make long sweeping strokes down both arms, from shoulder to finger tips, torso, front and back, both legs from hip to ankles, head and neck. This method is quite effective and can really be done anywhere. If I am in a place where it wouldn't be prudent to announce that I am brushing off dirty energy, I simply act like I am brushing off dog hair, or dust, or a spider web. No big deal.

Stay hydrated: That's pretty straightforward. Drink plenty of water. No, the water in beer, wine, and coffee doesn't really count. I follow the advice of drinking half my bodyweight in ounces per day. Find what numbers work best for you, but drink water.

Go outside: Ever heard the saying, "I'm going to take a walk to clear my head?" What people are really doing is clearing their energy, allowing them to think clearly. So, take a brisk walk. It doesn't have to be long or strenuous; five minutes will do. Getting outside in the fresh air, sunshine, and even the rain acts as a cleansing agent for our energy. **We are created from and designed to live amongst the universe, after all; it knows its part to play.**

Exercise | Choose a Cleansing Practice and Use It As Needed.

Look over the methods above or check out some of the amazing authors I recommended in the first part of this section, and find something that you are drawn to.

Plan to use your chosen cleansing method(s) before, during, or after specific events in the day, and any time that is needed in between. As I mentioned above, I end my day with a cleansing shower, which allows me to rest well and be ready for the next day — without carrying over debris from day to day.

I love thrift stores and garage sales. While I am shopping, I like to touch things, and after I touch something, I *always* brush my hands off. Even if I am not thrift shopping, if I touch something that leaves energetic debris, I simply brush it off.
It is much like washing our hands, we don't necessarily have a scheduled time that we do it, but we know which situations call for it.

Pulling it all together

The Mindful Energy Method is a simple, practical, and powerful combination of presence, energy, and intuition. When put to use, we can catch the wave of life-changing momentum.

The present time is all we ever have. Let's live there and be present there, meeting each moment that comes with openness and wonder. When we choose to be present we allow the subtle voice of intuition to be heard. We can take advantage of the task at hand, as it is happening, without the interference of stale or destructive beliefs. Being present encourages us to live with intention and attention, allowing for meaningful progress in all areas of our lives, while creating space for our intuitive knowing to be heard. In choosing to hear, trust, and act upon our inner knowing we increase our ability to solve problems, make decisions, and be creative. Our intuitive knowing is strengthened by proper care and nourishment of our energy body. When we attend to our energy body, we are able to be clear, focused and non-reactive in all of our life areas.

Bringing these three areas together is a powerful catalyst for change.

Now that this is all fresh in your mind, let's get to work!

MINDFUL ENERGY

A Journey of Self Transformation

Journal Section

There is a difference between knowing and doing. Now that you *know*, attention must be paid to what you *do*, by retraining your thought habits. That is the purpose of this next section — the journal. Every day you must attend to your thoughts, listen to your intuition, and engage with your energy.

Take time each day to read, reflect on, and answer the given questions. Make note of inspirations, a-ha moments, intuitions, and goals.

Using this journal is a way to show up and start being intentional about how you live — leaning into your own knowing, your own power. By acting upon what you have learned here, you set the stage for changing how you interact in the world and how the world interacts with you.

I'm **excited** to see what your journey brings! Visit www.mindfulenergybysarah.com to share your story.

Am I present today? Meeting each thing as it comes?

Have I made any aspect of any situation bigger or smaller than it really is?

Am I feeling my own feelings today? Or am I feeling other people's feelings for them?

Am I taking time to breathe deeply throughout the day?

Am I listening to my inner knowing — my gut feeling?

What am I grateful for?

NOTES

Am I present today? Meeting each thing as it comes?

Have I made any aspect of any situation bigger or smaller than it really is?

Am I feeling my own feelings today? Or am I feeling other people's feelings for them?

Am I taking time to breathe deeply throughout the day?

Am I listening to my inner knowing — my gut feeling?

What am I grateful for?

NOTES

Am I present today? Meeting each thing as it comes?

Have I made any aspect of any situation bigger or smaller than it really is?

Am I feeling my own feelings today? Or am I feeling other people's feelings for them?

Am I taking time to breathe deeply throughout the day?

Am I listening to my inner knowing — my gut feeling?

What am I grateful for?

NOTES

Am I present today? Meeting each thing as it comes?

Have I made any aspect of any situation bigger or smaller than it really is?

Am I feeling my own feelings today? Or am I feeling other people's feelings for them?

Am I taking time to breathe deeply throughout the day?

Am I listening to my inner knowing — my gut feeling?

What am I grateful for?

NOTES

Am I present today? Meeting each thing as it comes?

Have I made any aspect of any situation bigger or smaller than it really is?

Am I feeling my own feelings today? Or am I feeling other people's feelings for them?

Am I taking time to breathe deeply throughout the day?

Am I listening to my inner knowing — my gut feeling?

What am I grateful for?

NOTES

Am I present today? Meeting each thing as it comes?

Have I made any aspect of any situation bigger or smaller than it really is?

Am I feeling my own feelings today? Or am I feeling other people's feelings for them?

Am I taking time to breathe deeply throughout the day?

Am I listening to my inner knowing — my gut feeling?

What am I grateful for?

NOTES

Am I present today? Meeting each thing as it comes?

Have I made any aspect of any situation bigger or smaller than it really is?

Am I feeling my own feelings today? Or am I feeling other people's feelings for them?

Am I taking time to breathe deeply throughout the day?

Am I listening to my inner knowing — my gut feeling?

What am I grateful for?

NOTES

Am I present today? Meeting each thing as it comes?

Have I made any aspect of any situation bigger or smaller than it really is?

Am I feeling my own feelings today? Or am I feeling other people's feelings for them?

Am I taking time to breathe deeply throughout the day?

Am I listening to my inner knowing — my gut feeling?

What am I grateful for?

NOTES

Am I present today? Meeting each thing as it comes?

Have I made any aspect of any situation bigger or smaller than it really is?

Am I feeling my own feelings today? Or am I feeling other people's feelings for them?

Am I taking time to breathe deeply throughout the day?

Am I listening to my inner knowing — my gut feeling?

What am I grateful for?

NOTES

Am I present today? Meeting each thing as it comes?

Have I made any aspect of any situation bigger or smaller than it really is?

Am I feeling my own feelings today? Or am I feeling other people's feelings for them?

Am I taking time to breathe deeply throughout the day?

Am I listening to my inner knowing — my gut feeling?

What am I grateful for?

NOTES

Am I present today? Meeting each thing as it comes?

Have I made any aspect of any situation bigger or smaller than it really is?

Am I feeling my own feelings today? Or am I feeling other people's feelings for them?

Am I taking time to breathe deeply throughout the day?

Am I listening to my inner knowing — my gut feeling?

What am I grateful for?

NOTES

Am I present today? Meeting each thing as it comes?

Have I made any aspect of any situation bigger or smaller than it really is?

Am I feeling my own feelings today? Or am I feeling other people's feelings for them?

Am I taking time to breathe deeply throughout the day?

Am I listening to my inner knowing — my gut feeling?

What am I grateful for?

NOTES

Am I present today? Meeting each thing as it comes?

Have I made any aspect of any situation bigger or smaller than it really is?

Am I feeling my own feelings today? Or am I feeling other people's feelings for them?

Am I taking time to breathe deeply throughout the day?

Am I listening to my inner knowing — my gut feeling?

What am I grateful for?

NOTES

Am I present today? Meeting each thing as it comes?

Have I made any aspect of any situation bigger or smaller than it really is?

Am I feeling my own feelings today? Or am I feeling other people's feelings for them?

Am I taking time to breathe deeply throughout the day?

Am I listening to my inner knowing — my gut feeling?

What am I grateful for?

NOTES

Am I present today? Meeting each thing as it comes?

Have I made any aspect of any situation bigger or smaller than it really is?

Am I feeling my own feelings today? Or am I feeling other people's feelings for them?

Am I taking time to breathe deeply throughout the day?

Am I listening to my inner knowing — my gut feeling?

What am I grateful for?

NOTES

Am I present today? Meeting each thing as it comes?

Have I made any aspect of any situation bigger or smaller than it really is?

Am I feeling my own feelings today? Or am I feeling other people's feelings for them?

Am I taking time to breathe deeply throughout the day?

Am I listening to my inner knowing — my gut feeling?

What am I grateful for?

NOTES

Am I present today? Meeting each thing as it comes?

Have I made any aspect of any situation bigger or smaller than it really is?

Am I feeling my own feelings today? Or am I feeling other people's feelings for them?

Am I taking time to breathe deeply throughout the day?

Am I listening to my inner knowing — my gut feeling?

What am I grateful for?

NOTES

Am I present today? Meeting each thing as it comes?

Have I made any aspect of any situation bigger or smaller than it really is?

Am I feeling my own feelings today? Or am I feeling other people's feelings for them?

Am I taking time to breathe deeply throughout the day?

Am I listening to my inner knowing — my gut feeling?

What am I grateful for?

NOTES

Am I present today? Meeting each thing as it comes?

Have I made any aspect of any situation bigger or smaller than it really is?

Am I feeling my own feelings today? Or am I feeling other people's feelings for them?

Am I taking time to breathe deeply throughout the day?

Am I listening to my inner knowing — my gut feeling?

What am I grateful for?

NOTES

Am I present today? Meeting each thing as it comes?

Have I made any aspect of any situation bigger or smaller than it really is?

Am I feeling my own feelings today? Or am I feeling other people's feelings for them?

Am I taking time to breathe deeply throughout the day?

Am I listening to my inner knowing — my gut feeling?

What am I grateful for?

NOTES

Am I present today? Meeting each thing as it comes?

Have I made any aspect of any situation bigger or smaller than it really is?

Am I feeling my own feelings today? Or am I feeling other people's feelings for them?

Am I taking time to breathe deeply throughout the day?

Am I listening to my inner knowing — my gut feeling?

What am I grateful for?

NOTES

Am I present today? Meeting each thing as it comes?

Have I made any aspect of any situation bigger or smaller than it really is?

Am I feeling my own feelings today? Or am I feeling other people's feelings for them?

Am I taking time to breathe deeply throughout the day?

Am I listening to my inner knowing — my gut feeling?

What am I grateful for?

NOTES

Am I present today? Meeting each thing as it comes?

Have I made any aspect of any situation bigger or smaller than it really is?

Am I feeling my own feelings today? Or am I feeling other people's feelings for them?

Am I taking time to breathe deeply throughout the day?

Am I listening to my inner knowing — my gut feeling?

What am I grateful for?

NOTES

Am I present today? Meeting each thing as it comes?

Have I made any aspect of any situation bigger or smaller than it really is?

Am I feeling my own feelings today? Or am I feeling other people's feelings for them?

Am I taking time to breathe deeply throughout the day?

Am I listening to my inner knowing — my gut feeling?

What am I grateful for?

NOTES

Am I present today? Meeting each thing as it comes?

Have I made any aspect of any situation bigger or smaller than it really is?

Am I feeling my own feelings today? Or am I feeling other people's feelings for them?

Am I taking time to breathe deeply throughout the day?

Am I listening to my inner knowing — my gut feeling?

What am I grateful for?

NOTES

Am I present today? Meeting each thing as it comes?

Have I made any aspect of any situation bigger or smaller than it really is?

Am I feeling my own feelings today? Or am I feeling other people's feelings for them?

Am I taking time to breathe deeply throughout the day?

Am I listening to my inner knowing — my gut feeling?

What am I grateful for?

NOTES

Am I present today? Meeting each thing as it comes?

Have I made any aspect of any situation bigger or smaller than it really is?

Am I feeling my own feelings today? Or am I feeling other people's feelings for them?

Am I taking time to breathe deeply throughout the day?

Am I listening to my inner knowing — my gut feeling?

What am I grateful for?

NOTES

Am I present today? Meeting each thing as it comes?

Have I made any aspect of any situation bigger or smaller than it really is?

Am I feeling my own feelings today? Or am I feeling other people's feelings for them?

Am I taking time to breathe deeply throughout the day?

Am I listening to my inner knowing — my gut feeling?

What am I grateful for?

NOTES

Am I present today? Meeting each thing as it comes?

Have I made any aspect of any situation bigger or smaller than it really is?

Am I feeling my own feelings today? Or am I feeling other people's feelings for them?

Am I taking time to breathe deeply throughout the day?

Am I listening to my inner knowing — my gut feeling?

What am I grateful for?

NOTES

Am I present today? Meeting each thing as it comes?

Have I made any aspect of any situation bigger or smaller than it really is?

Am I feeling my own feelings today? Or am I feeling other people's feelings for them?

Am I taking time to breathe deeply throughout the day?

Am I listening to my inner knowing — my gut feeling?

What am I grateful for?

NOTES

Am I present today? Meeting each thing as it comes?

Have I made any aspect of any situation bigger or smaller than it really is?

Am I feeling my own feelings today? Or am I feeling other people's feelings for them?

Am I taking time to breathe deeply throughout the day?

Am I listening to my inner knowing — my gut feeling?

What am I grateful for?

NOTES

Am I present today? Meeting each thing as it comes?

Have I made any aspect of any situation bigger or smaller than it really is?

Am I feeling my own feelings today? Or am I feeling other people's feelings for them?

Am I taking time to breathe deeply throughout the day?

Am I listening to my inner knowing — my gut feeling?

What am I grateful for?

NOTES

Am I present today? Meeting each thing as it comes?

Have I made any aspect of any situation bigger or smaller than it really is?

Am I feeling my own feelings today? Or am I feeling other people's feelings for them?

Am I taking time to breathe deeply throughout the day?

Am I listening to my inner knowing — my gut feeling?

What am I grateful for?

NOTES

Am I present today? Meeting each thing as it comes?

Have I made any aspect of any situation bigger or smaller than it really is?

Am I feeling my own feelings today? Or am I feeling other people's feelings for them?

Am I taking time to breathe deeply throughout the day?

Am I listening to my inner knowing — my gut feeling?

What am I grateful for?

NOTES

Am I present today? Meeting each thing as it comes?

Have I made any aspect of any situation bigger or smaller than it really is?

Am I feeling my own feelings today? Or am I feeling other people's feelings for them?

Am I taking time to breathe deeply throughout the day?

Am I listening to my inner knowing — my gut feeling?

What am I grateful for?

NOTES

Am I present today? Meeting each thing as it comes?

Have I made any aspect of any situation bigger or smaller than it really is?

Am I feeling my own feelings today? Or am I feeling other people's feelings for them?

Am I taking time to breathe deeply throughout the day?

Am I listening to my inner knowing — my gut feeling?

What am I grateful for?

NOTES

Am I present today? Meeting each thing as it comes?

Have I made any aspect of any situation bigger or smaller than it really is?

Am I feeling my own feelings today? Or am I feeling other people's feelings for them?

Am I taking time to breathe deeply throughout the day?

Am I listening to my inner knowing — my gut feeling?

What am I grateful for?

NOTES

Am I present today? Meeting each thing as it comes?

Have I made any aspect of any situation bigger or smaller than it really is?

Am I feeling my own feelings today? Or am I feeling other people's feelings for them?

Am I taking time to breathe deeply throughout the day?

Am I listening to my inner knowing — my gut feeling?

What am I grateful for?

NOTES

Am I present today? Meeting each thing as it comes?

Have I made any aspect of any situation bigger or smaller than it really is?

Am I feeling my own feelings today? Or am I feeling other people's feelings for them?

Am I taking time to breathe deeply throughout the day?

Am I listening to my inner knowing — my gut feeling?

What am I grateful for?

NOTES

Am I present today? Meeting each thing as it comes?

Have I made any aspect of any situation bigger or smaller than it really is?

Am I feeling my own feelings today? Or am I feeling other people's feelings for them?

Am I taking time to breathe deeply throughout the day?

Am I listening to my inner knowing — my gut feeling?

What am I grateful for?

NOTES

Am I present today? Meeting each thing as it comes?

Have I made any aspect of any situation bigger or smaller than it really is?

Am I feeling my own feelings today? Or am I feeling other people's feelings for them?

Am I taking time to breathe deeply throughout the day?

Am I listening to my inner knowing — my gut feeling?

What am I grateful for?

NOTES

Am I present today? Meeting each thing as it comes?

Have I made any aspect of any situation bigger or smaller than it really is?

Am I feeling my own feelings today? Or am I feeling other people's feelings for them?

Am I taking time to breathe deeply throughout the day?

Am I listening to my inner knowing — my gut feeling?

What am I grateful for?

NOTES

Am I present today? Meeting each thing as it comes?

Have I made any aspect of any situation bigger or smaller than it really is?

Am I feeling my own feelings today? Or am I feeling other people's feelings for them?

Am I taking time to breathe deeply throughout the day?

Am I listening to my inner knowing — my gut feeling?

What am I grateful for?

NOTES

Am I present today? Meeting each thing as it comes?

Have I made any aspect of any situation bigger or smaller than it really is?

Am I feeling my own feelings today? Or am I feeling other people's feelings for them?

Am I taking time to breathe deeply throughout the day?

Am I listening to my inner knowing — my gut feeling?

What am I grateful for?

NOTES

Am I present today? Meeting each thing as it comes?

Have I made any aspect of any situation bigger or smaller than it really is?

Am I feeling my own feelings today? Or am I feeling other people's feelings for them?

Am I taking time to breathe deeply throughout the day?

Am I listening to my inner knowing — my gut feeling?

What am I grateful for?

NOTES

About The Author

Sarah is a speaker, teacher, life coach, intuitive, and creator of The Mindful Energy Method. She has spent more than fifteen years helping people achieve their goals. In that time, she has diligently studied the human process of failure and success, allowing for innovative insight and creation of proven methods for powerful transformation.

Sarah lives in the Pacific Northwest with her husband and three kids. When she's not working, she enjoys exploring the Oregon coast, reading, and cooking for friends and family.

Keep in touch with Sarah and stay up to date on all the latest events by visiting
www.mindfulenergybysarah.com